Love Is

30 Days

To Improving Your Relationship Communication

Learn How To Nurture A Deeper Love By Mastering The Art of Heart-To-Heart Relationship Communication

Table Of Contents

Introduction

Have you ever noticed how often people say they wish they could "find" love? As if love were something beautiful to just stumble upon on the side of the road. Yet when you speak to happily married couples, especially those that have been married for decades, they never ascribe their success and happiness to luck. Instead, they'll probably tell you that a good relationship takes work - lots of it - and the continued effort and maintenance from both sides.

Love is a *verb*.

It is not something only some people are fortunate enough to catch and then merely set aside. It's not a prize you win or a box to tick on your life's checklist. Instead, love has to be kindled and rebuilt *every day*; it has to be invited in, nurtured, cultivated. Love is not something passive that you simply have or don't have - it's an active process and the continual expression of what's in your heart, mind and soul.

In this book, love is not a noun. It isn't some mysterious gift from the gods that falls into our laps, but something that we can work on and build with intention. So, in that spirit, this book will not be a dispassionate list of relationship advice, or theories about the way people work together, or tips to heat up your sex life.

Instead, this book will ask you to become *actively* involved, to not just read but to constantly apply what has been read to your own life. And since we are on the topic of heart-to-heart communication, you're naturally going to need to rope in your partner, too. The exercises are experiential, meaning, simply, that you have to actually *do* them in order to benefit from them.

You'll be asked to be honest with yourself, get out there into the world and even make yourself vulnerable. Some of these exercises will be fun, others will scare and challenge you - but they are all designed to open your heart to more effective communication with others, so that the relationships you build are strong, heart centered and compassionate.

This book is written for anyone who feels that they are not living (and loving!) to their full potential. Whether you crave deeper connections with others or want to reignite relationships you are already in, this book was written to help you master the art of good communication.

In fact, it would be ideal for you to think of this book itself as one of the first of many new and interesting conversations you're going to have. Although I don't know you and cannot be sure of your response to what's written in these pages, I want for to engage with and respond to everything here as though I was sitting right there in the room with you.

You don't have to agree with everything, or like the principles outlined here. The important thing, though, is that in opening up the dialogue, you are already taking those first few steps to becoming more conscious, compassionate lovers and partners.

When we risk nothing, we gain nothing. When we don't open ourselves to love, we don't love deeply. My wish is that this book leaves you feeling open and receptive to love - your own ability to give it as well as the privilege of receiving it. And I hope that you have high expectations for yourself in reading it, too.

When two people come together, in any capacity, there is the chance for something special to happen. Every great romance began with a meeting of two hearts, with the first word of the first conversation. Let's begin this book with the first word. I am pleased to meet you, dear reader, and hope that in moving through this book together, we can jointly create a little more love, a little more tenderness and a little more understanding in the world than there was to begin with.

Chapter 1: Map of a Dysfunctional Relationship

Well, it may be a strange place to start, but let's begin our conversation with all those ways relationships *don't* work. If you're reading this book, chances are you've had difficulty with relationships in the past, or are currently unhappy in your situation. You can find plenty of information out there on codependent relationships, on partners who abuse, on relationships built around jealousy and guilt, and much more.

But perhaps all "bad" relationships, whatever their particular challenges, have some common elements. Here are ten characteristics of a style of relating with others that may be destructive, counterproductive or even dangerous. You'll notice that what makes a bad relationship is not the behavior or the individuals that make it, but *the pattern of relating* between them.

As you prepare to start your 30 days, use these beginning chapters to try and map out your challenging areas - just be receptive: if you notice any strong feelings for a particular topic, make a note. After each characteristic, answer the questions and see if some of these themes resonate with you.

In dysfunctional relationships, affection is a zero sum game

Everyone has 24 hours in their day, a finite amount of money in their bank accounts and only so many seats in their car. For most things in life, an increase on one side means taking away from the other side. In other words, it's "zero sum".

But love isn't like this. There is no need for a scarcity mentality when it comes to love and affection for others, because love is not a quantity that you can count or run out of. Think about it now: after spending quality time with those you love, after caring for them and lashing plenty of affection and attention on them, do you feel like you've "spent" all your love and now it's finished?

Of course not. If anything, the more love you give, the more love there is to give.

An unhealthy relationship treats warmth, affection and kindness as if they were measurable substances that can be given, earned or even bartered with. What else is jealousy but the fear that should somebody else receive love, there will somehow be less of it available for you?

Jealousy is damaging in relationships because it puts us in a fearful instead of thankful mindset. When we are jealous, we turn our attention to being defensive against perceived dangers, instead of enjoying what we do have.

Of course, jealousy doesn't only manifest in the form of fear of other people. Everyone knows that jealous partner who can't seem to let their boyfriend or girlfriend enjoy their lives without them being involved. Whether it's a hobby, family commitments or work, a jealous partner will be threatened if the object of their affection experiences happiness that doesn't come directly from them.

The problem with this way of thinking is that it shuts off the ability to see how much love and affection there is around us at all times. Intense and possessive partners can become so wrapped up in their beloved that they forget that there is a whole world out there, and that it doesn't really make sense to fearfully hold onto one "source" of love as if it was the only one.

Do you have any of the following beliefs about love? Be honest and tick all that apply.

- I feel like love is something I have to earn by working hard to get it

- I don't want to *ever* hear about my partner's exes - I hate that they've been with other people.

- A bad relationship is better than none at all.

- I feel that if my partner were to be attracted to someone else, it would immediately invalidate their attraction to me.

- I believe in soul mates.

In dysfunctional relationships, vulnerability is used as a weapon

In every relationship, people need to lower their defensive veils and take the risk of truly connecting with another person. And when we make that love connection, we're even more vulnerable: a person we love can hurt us so much more than anyone else.

But the risk is worth it - and of course it is, considering how many people take the plunge over and over again. Opening up to someone else can be so beautiful precisely *because* we are vulnerable - and loved anyway.

In an unhealthy relationship, people use one another's vulnerability to their own advantage. Gentleness, affection and the willingness to share deep and intimate parts of yourself are merely seen as tools to hurt the other if it comes down to it.

You've heard this story before: a woman, repeatedly beaten and mistreated by her husband, claims she could never leave him. Why? Because she loves him. Her love for her husband is not seen as a precious thing to be protected and nurtured, but as a means to have power over her, a tool of manipulation.

For many people, openly admitting feelings, confessing desires and sharing their deepest selves is more or less the same thing as weakness - a weakness to be exploited. Relationships where vulnerability is not cherished are easy to spot: communication is based on warped power dynamics, abuse of "authority" and manipulation take the place of compassion.

Abusive relationships of all kinds fall into this category, but so do partners who seemingly keep each other at arm's length for years. Denying your partner sexual intimacy as a punishment, threatening to leave unless you get your way, using guilt to get them to do what you want - all of these are ways of taking what should be a tender and safe space and turning it into a battleground.

Do you have some of these beliefs?

- If you don't ever trust people, then you can never get hurt.

- If someone loves me, then it's their responsibility to keep me happy and give me what I need.

- I often feel humiliated and used after a breakup.

- It's better to find someone who loves you more than you love them.

- In fights, I know exactly what to say and do to push my partner's buttons.

In dysfunctional relationships, people compete rather than cooperate

As teenagers, our main challenge in life is to sort ourselves out - find our identities, refine what we believe in and work on our own life code and worldview. Adulthood is different, however. Assuming our sense of self is more or less settled, we're expected to start caring more about others the older we get.

By becoming parents, we forever give up ourselves as the main focus of our attention and learn to take into account someone else's well being - the child's. Even if you're never a parent, though, there comes a time as an adult when you need to build collaborative relationships with others.

In partnered relationships, there is necessarily a degree of compromise. By working as a team on shared goals, a couple can achieve and experience so much more than otherwise.

Unhealthy relationships, however, lack this sense of cooperation. When both partners merely see the other as an extension of their own individual life plan, as a means to an end or even someone to directly compete with, the partnership can never be a collaboration.

People who aren't interested in or supportive of their partner's success and failure, those who don't actively try to be a part of their partner's dreams and goals, those that insist on maintaining the lifestyle they had when they were single and simply expect the other to adapt - these partners are not working together with their partner but *against* them.

Do you have any of these beliefs?

- It's not my problem if my partner fails at something.

- I get uncomfortable if my partner always performs better than me.

- When we fight, it's always about getting each other to comply with the other one's idea of what's right.

- Major life decisions are mine to make and have nothing to do with my partner.

- I sometimes feel very smothered by my partner.

In dysfunctional relationships, there is no deep recognition of each other's being

Happy, long term couples look at one another, warts and all, and embrace the full package. It sort of goes without saying but a healthy relationship is one where two people... actually like one another.

Dysfunctional relationships are characterized by a complete and utter disregard for the very things that make your partner who they are. A person's personality, heart, mind and soul are not dishes at a buffet that you can pick and choose from. Loving one part and hating another does a great disservice to your partner.

Of course, loving partners know when to call the other on their bad behavior, and they don't tolerate it. But *acceptance* of what your partner's weaknesses are communicates that your love is not half-baked, but applies to *all* of them.

Maybe you know a couple who are like this. Their irritation with one another goes deeper than niggles over bad habits - it seems to go to the very core of the person's being. When you don't respect and accept what makes your partner who they are, there simply just isn't room for a healthy relationship to develop.

This may seem obvious to some people, but less obvious perhaps is the fact that many nurture relationships in which there is no active appreciation of one another, even though there is the absence of actual hostility. Does your partner think you're awesome? Do you really *like* them, as people?

In some relationships, the practical or physical benefits of a union can become so much a point of focus that everyone forgets that they were meant to really, truly and on a deep level, approve of their partners.

Relationships where there is a lack of affirmation of one another will leave both feeling drained and uninvested. Such a relationship always feels like an uphill battle - the kind of ordeal that has you asking, what's the point?

Do you have any of the following beliefs?

- My partner doesn't really "get" me as a person.

- There are some values my partner has or choices he or she has made that I simply don't respect.

- I think there are definite ways my partner could improve themselves that would make them easier to love.

- We spend a lot of time negotiating and criticizing each other.

- I'm often disappointed with my partner for not meeting my expectations.

- I feel like I could probably do better.

Dysfunctional relationships are fear based

"Why don't you leave her?"
"I don't know what I'd do without her."

In an unhealthy relationship, the driving force behind the connection is *negative*. The union may not be that great, for example, but it's better than nothing. Rather than cherished for what it is, this kind of relationship's best feature is what it *isn't*. Compare the above with:

"Why don't you leave her?"
"I love spending time with her. She makes everything so much lighter and happier."

There are plenty of things that keep people locked into relationships that are objectively not so great. It could be the fact that you are afraid of the financial ramifications of divorcing, or you're afraid of what your friends and family will think of you if you're single at your particular age, or you're afraid that your partner will be a miserable failure without you.

Maybe you're afraid you'll never find anyone else, or you're afraid that your partner will seek revenge or worse, harm you physically, or you're just afraid of having to start dating again if you had to break up. Whatever the reason, all of these are rooted in fear and not in the benefits you actually get from staying together. It could be the worst relationship in the world, but as long as it's better than the alternative, it's tolerated.

Do you have any of these beliefs?

- I can't imagine anyone else ever finding me attractive.

- My relationship benefits those around me more than it benefits me.

- I'm with my partner because I depend on them completely.

- I've thought a lot about ending my relationship but never do.

- Sometimes, you just have to settle.

Of course, you may be able to identify many more themes common to dysfunctional relationships - perhaps even some that apply to you directly. Take a moment to reflect on what you think are your most prominent relationship challenges. At the end of the day, in unhealthy connections, people bring out the worst, and not the best in one another.

Chapter 2: What is a Heart-Centered Relationship?

In the book Anna Karenina, Tolstoy says that all happy families are all alike, but unhappy families are unhappy in their own completely unique ways. I think relationships are similar. No matter the details, happy, heart centered and compassionate couples work from a basis of love, respect and honesty in the way they relate to one another. Here are some characteristics of such relationships.

Respect

Never calling your partner names, belittling them or undermining the value of what they believe and do. Taking their projects seriously and valuing their insight and input during conversations. A respected partner is not even necessarily one that you always agree with, only that you respect their ability to hold different opinions.

Honesty

Without trust, there can be no real depth of connection. Honest partners go above and beyond simply refraining from lying, they actively try to be transparent with their partners, communicating their experience and not hiding things that their partner would prefer to know. Honest partners don't support each other's denial, either, and expect that for any meaningful communication to happen, everyone needs to be on the same page.

You may say, sure, I'm honest, I've never tried to deceive my partner, but sometimes this isn't enough. Have you wrangled the truth a little to serve your own needs, even if not directly lying? Is there something that would be better if said instead of just assumed?

Trust

On the flip side, relationships with heart do not operate with mistrust and suspicion. In a healthy partnership, someone is innocent until proven guilty. Trust is given freely and not as some sort of reward or bonus. Partners assume the best of each other and have no need to snoop on them or demand they prove their loyalty.

Encouragement

The right partner will love to see you happy and successful. They'll push you to be the best version of yourself, because they believe in you. This kind of love is selfless - such a partner cares about what you're doing with your life for no reason other than that they want you to live well. Partners who are each other's cheerleaders will never be alone when it comes to weathering life's difficulties.

Variety and spontaneity

It's easy to be endlessly fascinated with your partner in the early days. Later on, when they are less of a mystery to you, you'll both need to take deliberate action to maintain the proverbial spice of life. Routine is death for a relationship. In a strong, healthy relationship, both partners constantly strive to try to new things, go places, learn things and rediscover their partner over and over again. It may sound like a bit of a paradox, but spontaneity is something that can be planned and controlled!

Boundaries

Though we've seen how important it is to work as a team, a relationship needs well-defined boundaries on both sides. You need to know exactly where you draw the line and know how to calmly and reasonably assert that boundary if it gets crossed. Maintaining a strong personal identity means there's more to bring to your partner when you do connect. Happy partners know when they begin and where their partner ends - and they take responsibility for the their actions.

The list could go on an on; love, passion, romance, good communication skills, plenty of fun activities, a life away from your partner, shared goals etc. etc.

Ultimately, a heart centered relationship is one that acknowledges and affirms both partners at their very core, with compassion and acceptance. A relationship is strong when it draws on the fact that both partners sincerely want the best for the other - they don't want their partner to be who they aren't, or to be whatever would benefit *them* the most, but to be a congruent, fulfilled and happy individual.

Heartfelt compassion doesn't cling or demand, it isn't panicky and insecure, needing to be propped up by outside affection. This kind of love is big and expansive, growing and changing as each partner develops, built on solid communication, honesty and genuine desire for the happiness of the other.

A mature, heart-centered relationship is a thing of beauty - light, warm and a source of energy and inspiration. Sounds good, doesn't it?

Take some time now to reflect on some of your most deeply held beliefs about what love is and isn't. Here are some questions to guide your exploration of your own personal mythology, your own store of memories, dreams, hopes and fears when it comes to love.

- What do you most want from you partner - and when was the last time you gave that to someone else?

- What would you say to an alien from outer space who landed on earth and asked you what 'love' was?

- What is missing from where your life is now to where you want it to be?

- At the end of the day, what is your passion in life?

Chapter 3: The Art of Communication

What is a relationship other than a long string of small conversations?

Every time you reach out to your partner or shut them off, when you choose to use certain words and not others, when you smile or turn your body away from them, even when you are completely silent - you are communicating.

Communication is that strange interface, that curious place in between two people where they must find a way to bridge the gap. Of course communication is not just verbal. When we reach out in any way, when we try to make ourselves understood or when we try to understand others, we are attempting to communicate.

We can make our intentions known through the way we use our bodies, our words, our facial expressions, and our actions. When we communicate with someone else, we are temporarily inviting them to become a part of our experience. We're saying, *listen to me! What I have to say is important.*

When we communicate properly, a healthy and happy relationship naturally follows. And why not? When both partners know what the other is experiencing, when everyone understand the mutual goals and expectations, when fights are sorted out before they even begin, a relationship cannot help but be a successful one.

But, this is easier said than done. "Conscious" communication is choosing to become aware of the messages we are sending to our partner, to ourselves and out into the world in general. Becoming more perceptive means we can also tune into the messages of those around us, hearing what is actually said rather than what we wish was said.

How can you become a more conscious communicator?

The answer is simple: pay attention. Pay attention to what is happening inside your own heart and mind. Notice the rise and fall of emotions, thoughts that you have, notice unquestioning beliefs, fears and expectations.

Turn your antennae, too, towards the outside and really listen to what your partner is communicating. Even those who are not the most skilled of communicators know that when people say "I'm fine" with just the right tone of voice and body language, they actually mean exactly the opposite.

Learning to become more responsive, more aware and more in tune with yourself and others means you'll communicate your own needs better as well as understand others. You'll reduce the chance of misunderstandings or harmful assumptions.

Here are some smart ways to start being more deliberate in the way you communicate. Once you begin your 30 days, you may need to refer back to some of these skills and techniques to help reach your partner and express yourself. As you read, consider whether each particular skill is a strength or a challenge for you.

Acknowledge emotional content first

Here is a tip that many marriage counselors, divorce mediators and even hostage negotiators know how to use wisely: acknowledge the emotional content of what is said. People use words, sometimes a lot of words, but when people have conversations, there is always a more subtle undercurrent of emotional communication.

When you communicate to those close to you, make a point of hearing this emotional undercurrent as well as the words spoken. When you respond to this, you cut away the clutter and small talk - in a deeper way, you "hear" the person more fully.

A classic example is the woman who complains at the end of a long day to her partner. She tells him how irritating everyone was, how rude her clients, how naughty the children, how bad the traffic. Instead of hearing the exasperation and defeat in her voice (i.e. the emotional content) her partner only hears a string of complaints and problems. So, he sets to helping her solve them.

Had he responded to the emotional content first, he would have seen that the emotional message was, *I'm having a hard time, please sympathize with me.* When he instead responds, "Well, maybe you should take another route home from work if traffic is such a big deal" he is communicating to her that he hasn't "heard" properly at all. This misunderstanding likely just gets added to her list of the irritations of the day.

Instead, if he simply says something like, "Wow, you've had a lot to deal with today. Sit down, I'll make us some tea", the communication is instantly more conscious and compassionate.

Become familiar with different styles of communication

If you have not already, it's a great idea to read the book *The Five Love Languages* by Gary Chapman. Even when we believe we are expressing ourselves loud and clear, sometimes we are just on different "wavelengths" than our partners.

The five love languages, according to this book, are physical touch, acts of service, quality time, gifts and words of affirmation (food is also a suggested language). But you may have your own special blend of languages or require that people express their affection in particular ways.

While it's good to know your own preference, the trick is to make sure that you are communicating in the language that your *partner* prefers when you interact with them. You may choose to express affection through a hug or sex, or your partner may hear you clearest when you praise them and build up their self esteem with compliments and affirmations.

Your partner might notice your love the most when you help out around the house, do little chores for him to make his life easier or stand up for him in difficult moments. If their language of love is gifts, you would show your partner your love by regularly observing occasions with carefully planned gifts, taking them to dinner and surprising them with little trinkets or hidden notes.

In understanding what your own language is, you can learn to make reasonable and clear requests of your partner. Don't feel strange saying something like, "I love it when you X, it really makes me feel appreciated". Pay close attention to your partner's language, too, and you'll ensure that when you speak to them, the right channel is open.

Start smart conversations and survive "we need to talk"

As we've seen, a good relationship is a single, constant, flowing conversation, but once in a while you'll need to deliberately start a conversation with your partner, possibly a difficult one.

Step One: Sort out your intention

There's nothing worse than instigating a difficult conversation without clearly understanding exactly why you're doing it. Your partner will get that you are unhappy somehow, but without any focus and forethought, you may end up aggravating matters without coming to any conclusion.

Before you approach anyone to talk, figure out what you want. The first, and most important step, is to ask yourself what the purpose of the talk is, and exactly what you see as the end point. But be honest. Many people would say, "I want to express my feelings about such and so", which seems pretty innocuous, but on closer inspection, what they really want to do is blame someone, or even punish them. Be honest about ulterior motives.

Sometimes, when you examine your intention, you may discover that it's best not to say anything. Does your talk improve on the silence? Are there better ways to express yourself? Sometimes, as they say, actions speak louder than words. If you've identified a reasonable, heart centered goal that will be improved by speaking to your partner, go ahead to the next step.

Step Two: Identify the position of the other person

This is vital. To communicate, you always have to know whom you are communicating *to*. Here are some questions you can ask to zero in on the other person's perspective. Compare the answers to those you'd give for yourself.

- Are you making any assumptions about their position that are not strictly supported?

- What emotions have they communicated to you so far?

- Is there any chance you will be misinterpreted?

- How do you think you will be perceived and how can you make sure it's accurately conveyed?

- How do your goals compare with your partner's? How can you find out?

- What have you done to contribute to the problem you are bringing up?

- Can you anticipate the issues your partner will bring to the conversation?

Step Three: Begin like Socrates

In Socratic dialogue, you start any enquiry assuming you know absolutely nothing and are trying to learn. Clear your mind of assumptions and past experiences. Try to really listen. Imagine you are approaching the problem for the first time. Open a conversation by letting your partner speak first. Let them say everything they need to. Listen without thinking of what you'll say when they're done. Repeat what you heard back to them to confirm you have understood. Take it slow and give them ample room to express their side of things. Try to truly consider their perspective. Open with statements like:

- "There's something I wanted to talk about with you and I'm hoping it will help us communicate better."

- "I've really wanted to talk about X with you. First, I'd like to get your opinion on it."

- "It seems like we have different ideas about X, and I'd like to really understand why you think Y."

- "I would really appreciate if you could help me understand something I've been having trouble with..."

- "I really would like to share my perspective with you about X. Maybe you can tell me your feelings first?"

Remember to be respectful. Your first task is not to win someone over or convince them to accept your way. Initially, you are just trying to get a very thorough understanding of one another. A good technique is to be actively reflective as you talk: if you notice that the other person seems defensive, comment on it. Say something like, "I noticed that you seemed to get defensive just there. Am I right? I'm curious about what made you feel that way."

A good way to start with this sort of discussion is to constantly acknowledge and affirm the information coming from the other side. Say things like, "It seems to me that I feel X and you feel Y. Do you agree?" or "I can see that X means a lot to you. Let me explain why I don't agree..."

Step Four: Focus the discussion on solutions

The beginning of the discussion is the time to air and acknowledge everyone's feelings. However long this takes, each person should feel that they've had sufficient time to express themselves and that they have been heard. Don't feel awkward about saying things like, "Okay, it seems like you're saying X. Have I heard you correctly?" or, "I'd like to explain again, because I don't feel as though you've understood just yet..."

At a certain point, though, an issue is only resolved with realistic, action oriented discussion. The second half of the discussion should focus on rational solutions to the issues raised. A good thing to think of throughout the discussion is: in what ways do we want the same thing? Identify and build on this, for example, "I see we have different ideas, but fundamentally we both seem to want X. Maybe we can think together of ways to get X for both of us."

If conflict arises again, start back at step one. If you seem to be going in circles, it may be prudent to stop and assess whether the discussion may be better had later on when emotions have cooled. Here are some useful phrases that are heart centered and focused on finding workable solutions for everyone.

- "I understand what you're saying. I have often felt like that, too. However..."

- "I'm feeling very unhappy about this. I really want to resolve it because I am used to being honest and open with you and I don't want anything to disrupt that."

- "What can I do to make this easier for you?"

- "You make me very happy. I'd like to ask that you do X."

Life is complicated and confrontations like this, as much as we try, can often be awkward, gut wrenching and sometimes end quite badly. Remember, the price of affection we pay is the risk of rejection and hurt. Try to accept things gracefully and calmly. Take some time afterwards to process your emotions. If you're at a loss, a good compass to follow is: is this for your highest good? For the highest good of your partner?

Take responsibility and enforce your own boundaries

Responsibility and boundaries go hand in hand. In partnerships, it is our responsibility to erect meaningful emotional boundaries, and our partner's responsibility to respect them. It is our responsibility to enforce those boundaries when they are violated.

In romantic relationships, it can be hard to draw the line between what is ours, what is our partner's and what is shared in the relationship. Make a habit of sorting issues out into these categories. Here's an example.

Lets say a "we need to talk" conversation arises. John tells Beth that he has become increasingly bothered by her weight gain. Over the years, stress and lack of good diet and exercise have left her in poor shape, and he attempts to start a dialogue about it.

Beth, who has a history of disordered eating and is currently under a lot of stress at work, feels her self esteem is at rock bottom and is understandably hurt and humiliated at what John has to say.

Now, in this scenario, who is to "blame"? Where, exactly, is the source of the problem? In other words, what is Beth's, what is John's and what is both of theirs? Lets examine the boundaries and responsibilities of each.

John:

John has a right to find whatever he finds desirable, and the right to express that. His boundary takes the form of asserting that he cannot be attracted to what he isn't attracted to, and if Beth gains a significant amount of weight, he is put in an awkward position. He has a right to express that.

What he doesn't have a right to, however, is what Beth does with her body. He can merely express his own standard and preference - but his right stops at Beth's right to be however she wants to be. For John to assert a healthy boundary without violating the boundaries of Beth, he has to acknowledge this.

Beth:

Beth has a right to be stressed, to process her stress and to have difficulty in life. She has the right to struggle occasionally and the right to ask for sympathy and understanding while she does so. She can assert that boundary by demanding nothing but thoughtful respect from John.

What she doesn't have the right to, however, is John's unconditional attraction. She doesn't have any claim on what his experience is, or how he perceives her. While she is free to gain or lose weight or any other thing, John's reaction to this is entirely his own.

How can they both resolve the issue?

In any ensuing discussion, it is Beth's responsibility to own what's hers. She cannot accuse John of making her feel bad if she experiences low self esteem. That is hers and hers alone. Similarly, John can express himself freely when it comes to his feelings and expectations, but he can never demand that it's Beth's responsibility to give him that. He might prefer a skinny wife, but it is not Beth's responsibility to give it to him.

What is in both Beth and John's best interest? What addresses their highest good?

As they hash the situation out, they may discover that it's beneficial for both if Beth can have some sympathy and understanding while John encourages her to start living a healthier lifestyle. There is no blame, no expectation and entitlement, only a loving, realistic and compassionate working together on the problem.

Watch out for statements such as:

"You make me feel..."

Nobody *makes* you feel anything. You and only you decide how to feel about something. You are in charge of your own emotional response, and nobody can interfere with that - unless you give them permission to. Don't blame your choices - whether they are obvious actions or less obvious emotions - on someone else. Say instead, "I feel..."

"You should be more..."

You can have a preference for something. You can really wish something were the case. You can want with all your heart that the word be a certain way. But it doesn't entitle you to getting it. And it doesn't entitle you to demand it of your partner. Instead of saying, "You should be thoughtful!", say something like, "When you say things like that, I feel attacked."

It is your decision to feel attacked, and your partner's decision about whether to alter their behavior to accommodate you. Someone who doesn't respect your boundaries deserves no place in your life, but they should respect those boundaries because they want to, not because you tell them to.

"I'm sorry, I just..."

Whatever you feel, you feel. Don't make apologies for it or try to soften what you think and feel. Put it out there, and own it. Of course, your feelings don't entitle you to any particular claim on the world, but they are *yours*. Be proud of them. Assert your experience. Apologizing for the way you feel is like apologizing for digesting or breathing. You don't have to be sorry for what happens naturally. How you deal with those feelings, however, is completely under your conscious and deliberate control.

Chapter 4: Nurturing the Flame

We've had a look at the various characteristics of a healthy and a not-so-healthy relationship. But what if, like so many people in long-term relationships - everything is, well, just *fine*? You know what "fine" means: not bad enough to leave. Comfortable. OK. Tolerable.

You could communicate like champions, never fight and have a genuinely respectful and low-drama relationship - but then again, you may be more or less the same as two roommates who get on well.

Maybe human beings will never find a comfortable and permanent way to negotiate monogamy. Maybe love, no matter how good it starts out, eventually fades. For whatever reason, sometimes the zing just... disappears. It's not a matter of communication or being compassionate.

First things first: a relationship that doesn't last is not necessarily a failed one.

You can enjoy a meal, a ballet performance or a good novel even though there comes a time when it's finished. Just because it had a finite duration, doesn't mean it was worth any less. Having said that, our culture does put a premium on connections that last - and for sure relationships that go on for years have the chance to develop and mellow in ways shorter connections can't.

In many ways, finding love is not the most difficult - *keeping* love is. Flirting and catching the right kind of people is like the miracle of getting a seed to germinate - but a long-term commitment is like growing that seed into a massive tree, season after season, through winter and spring.

Here are some things to consider if your situation is, well - if it's fine. Just fine.

- Think of the way you dressed, spoke and behaved when you first met your partner. Do you do that still? Why not?

- In the last week, have you shared something new, interesting or entertaining with your partner? If you're always together, of course, you can never have exciting conversations about the developments in each other's lives.

- Make a commitment right now to stop gross "roommate behavior": close the bathroom door, refrain from belching or picking your teeth in front of them, throw away disgusting socks you routinely wear around the house and maintain good hygiene. There is a natural and comfortable set point that a couple reaches - but don't let it slide.

- Go on holiday. Leave behind chores and obligations and carve out a space where you can just enjoy each other for a while.

- Sometimes the best way to reinvigorate a stale relationship is to stop focusing on it at all. Have a break from each other, from talking about the relationship, from shared anything. Go out with friends, pursue hobbies. Then, bring that freshness back to your partner.

- Forget about it. Forget about all the things they've done, all the ways they're wrong. You don't need to forgive them, to hash it out, to punish them. Just forget it - really. Couples who have been through a few seasons know that sometimes, you just make the decision that you're going to get along, and that's the end of it.

- Dampened libidos and routine sex can be awful - why even have sex if it's going to be exactly what it was the previous 678 times? No matter how long you've known your partner, they are guaranteed to have some erotic terrain that you have not explored. Be playful and start a conversation about kinks or fantasies. Be naughty about it. Do something you've never done before.

- If it's something big, share it with your partner - don't let issues fester and poison the relationship. If they do something small to irritate you, do one of two things: call them out on it there and then, or forget it ever happened. Holding onto every little slight and crime is a recipe for resentment. Actively address it or let it go. The time to bring up your hurt feelings over something is not four months later during a fight about something else.

Long-term relationships have special challenges - see if you can identify your own particular issues before embarking on the 30 days. Before we start, lets take a quick look at one more issue that plagues many couples of all kinds.

Chapter 5: Love in the Time of Social Networks

Back in the day, you only knew the people who lived in your neighborhood and your immediate friends and family. Even further back in the day, you would likely only have ever encountered a small band of around 150 people at most who lived in your immediate tribe. The point is, for much of the history of the world, human beings never had the massive connectedness to one another that we do now.

The Internet and communication technology have meant that we have access to more people that we don't know than ever before. Think about this for a second. In the past, your average caveman would have *only* seen people he knew day in and day out. Today, walking on the streets, going about our lives, we encounter hundreds of people that we don't and won't ever know.

We may know more celebrities than we do actual people in our social circles. We have the strange new relationship category of "Facebook friend". At any time, we can reach out to people, strangers or otherwise, all over the world.

It's no surprise then, that the way we relate to one another and how we connect in relationships has also changed. Here are some ways to negotiate intimacy in an era of extreme connectedness, especially when it comes to social networks.

Don't assume - make boundaries clear

In the past, "thou shalt not covet or commit adultery" etc. was pretty much the sum total of the rules and regulations of most relationships. Today, the world is more complex. The only way to negotiate the new social landscape is to be explicit in your expectations and boundaries. Talk about it. What, exactly, do you consider infidelity? What counts as flirting?

Don't snoop

In the same way, respect your partner's boundaries. Don't poke around on their Facebook pages looking for "clues", don't guess their passwords, don't read over their shoulders and don't go through their browser history. Either you trust them, or you don't. Do be tempted to be one of those people who "accidentally stumbled" upon something upsetting. If you have suspicions or doubts, the person to speak to you is your partner.

Be congruent

It's easy to lead a double-life online. Make a point to conduct yourself online as you would offline. Don't leave room for misunderstandings or grey areas. If you are in a committed relationship, is that communicated in all the relevant places?

Maintain privacy

If it concerns your partner, think twice about sharing information online. You may have different ideas of what is appropriate to share in a public space. The whole point of a relationship is that at some point, there is something that belongs to the two of you and only to you two. Try not to over share when it comes to your relationship.

Chapter 6: Relationship Cardio: 30 Days to a Stronger Heart

Now that we've spent some time getting to grips with some fundamental communication strategies, it's time to put it all into practice. Most likely, you're reading this book because something, somehow in your relationship is not quite what you feel it could be. Perhaps you're onto the last straw of a long and difficult partnership and feel pretty close to giving up, or perhaps you've noticed the shine coming off what seemed to be a loving and close relationship.

Either way, the following exercises are designed to open up and initiate the kind of conversations that move you - and your partner - forward. Some of them will focus on your side of the dynamic exclusively - after all, this is one arena where you have the most control. But many will ask you to actively engage your partner.

What you'll need to begin your 30-day "relationship cardio":

- A sense of honesty, adventure and vulnerability - nothing worth it comes easy.

- A partner who is at least somewhat receptive

- A diary to record your thoughts, feelings and perceptions - buy a new and pretty notebook and start fresh on the first page (or, if it feels more appropriate, use a plain, humble notebook... just make sure you are reflecting and recording as you go...)

Day 1 - Catch up on your own housekeeping

Effective communication begins with someone who has something to communicate. This day is all about you. In your notebook, answer the following questions, and jot down any other feelings that emerge. There are no limits - be curious and accepting of what comes out.

- Would you date you? Why or why not?

- If you lived on an alien planet where people didn't even have relationships, what would your life look like?

- Today, are you the person you always hoped you'd be?

- If you had to summarize the essence of your life into just five words, what would those words be?

- Write down your wildest hopes and dreams for the end of the 30 days - what would success look like to you?

- Also write down your biggest fear in beginning this adventure. Be honest. You will have the chance to come back later and examine these fears and hopes.

Resist diagnosing anything or seeing patterns at this point - simply do a check-in on yourself and where you are in your life right now. Do yourself and your partner a favor and take stock today of your sense of self, your goals, your weak spots and what you want for the future.

Day 2 - Turn your antennae on

Today, you need to turn your curious attention outwards and onto the way you and your partner interact. Make notes of your emotions and thoughts, jot down the habits you engage in. In other words, try to make a summary, as if you were an outsider looking in, of what you see when you look at your relationship. Identify, as neutrally as possible, any sources of friction. At this point, you are still just collecting data. Whatever you notice, put it down in your journal. If you like, you may choose to even start recording your dreams at this time or add something creative and impressionistic to your journal: pictures, drawings or poems.

Day 3: Declare your intention

This may be a difficult day. If you've done your homework on yourself, you'll have a clearer idea of what you need from your partner and why. You cannot "fix" a relationship when only one person is working at improving it, however. Decide how you'll approach your partner and clarify before you do exactly what has motivated you to embark on improving the communication between you two. Be honest, compassionate and prepared. Record how you feel before and after. Give your partner time to respond.

Depending on the kind of relationship you have, your approach may be very different. You could casually bring it up and ask their opinion, or, if things are more adversarial, ask for some quiet time to address a few points. Notice any feelings of fear or resistance that come up. Do you feel guilty stating that you are unhappy? How does your partner's reaction make you feel? Note it all down. A good way to start is simply: "Hey, I've been reading a book about improving communication and I'm finding it quite interesting. I'd love to involve you in some of the exercises for the next month or so... what do you think?"

Day 4: Invite your partner to the conversation

Today, you are opening up channels. Depending on how yesterday went, you might feel more comfortable doing this. You've had the time to note down your feelings, fears and expectations, now extend the offer to your partner. Today, turn your attention to really hearing them, as much as you can. Your goal is to find out, are they happy? What makes them happy? Are they unhappy? Why?

After today, you should have a clarified idea of what both you and your partner believe to be your biggest relationship challenge. Don't try to argue or compare notes. Just open up and listen. Become a reporter, or a scientist. What are their expectations? Their fears? Try to communicate that you are receptive to whatever it is they have to say. If there is something that upsets you, put it aside for the time being and focus on trying to understand your partner's position fully.

Day 5: Breathing room

Every relationship is different. You may have discovered completely new and possibly upsetting information, or you may have found that speaking to your partner this way is stressful and leaves you feeling quite exposed. Today, just let whatever is, be what it is. Don't think about anything. Give your unconscious mind time to process. If you're depressed and hurt, just engage with it. Jot it all down. Allow your feelings to develop.

Day 6: Goal setting

In your notebook, write down three main goals that you have decided on. These goals can't be something like "I want her to be more X" but have to be goals for *you*. Make sure, also, that the goals can be achieved in 3 weeks or so, and that they are measurable - i.e. you'll know when they've been accomplished. Be realistic. Share these with your partner and encourage them to put down their own goals, if it feels right.

Day 7 to day 27: Your own program

The first week is about setting your intentions, making goals and establishing contact. The next 3 weeks are all about learning new ways to connect and communicate. Because no relationship is the same, it would be silly for everyone to follow the same formula. Instead, take a good look at your goals (and your partner's, if you know them).

Every day from now until day 27, you will pick one of the exercises below for each day. You'll be picking the exercises that relate to the issues your relationship faces as well as both of your goals. The following exercises fall into 4 categories (physical, lifestyle, communication, conflict).

Try not to do the same exercise more than 3 times, but if you find that it's particularly effective, do it again by all means. You might like to do each one once for a good variety.

At the end of each exercise, record in your journal what you have learnt about yourself, your partner and your relationship. Keep focused by returning to previous notes and your ultimate goals. Be gentle - this is a difficult and sometimes scary thing to do. Take a deep breath and keep taking notes.

Physical exercises

For when physical intimacy has faded, when you feel distant or that attraction is gone, or when your expectations and needs around sex do not align with your partner's.

The hug quotient

No matter what is going on in your lives, observe the "hug quotient". From now until the end of the thirty days, throw a dice each morning to determine the amount of non-negotiable hugs to be given to your partner, each of which lasts at least 30 seconds. Even if you're in the middle of a serious fight, do your hugs - no excuses.

No-sex sex

This is a technique prescribed by many sex therapists. Set aside a quiet evening where you can be physical with your partner. But actual sex is off the menu - do everything and anything that pleases your partner, but have no expectations and no direction - simply open up and become curious about how your bodies respond to each other.

The spa

Ask your partner what "spa treatments" they'd like: a massage, a foot rub, breakfast in bed? Devote yourself to them for an evening. Don't rush, just enjoy pampering them. Is it more difficult to give affection and pampering or receive it? What feelings come up when one partner's pleasure becomes the focus? And when things are reversed?

A romantic dinner

Go out somewhere fancy for a dinner. There's a twist though: don't speak about anything besides the restaurant experience. Compare, in detail, the tastes, sights, smells and sounds. Be fully present. Don't talk or think about anything for those few hours. Just let go and revel in the sumptuousness of both of your perceptions in the moment.

"Sexual favors"

For the rest of the month period, allot to both you and your partner 5 "sexual favors", where they can ask for what they would like without shame or rejection, and you can do the same. Make this as fun or as serious as you like. It can even be as simple as using one of your favors to request sex when the other partner isn't particularly interested. Note your reactions.

Love letters

Separately, you and your partner both compile a list of 5 things about the other that you find irresistible. Be flattering, raunchy or tender, you decide. Note the parts of their body you love the best, their smile, when they do X etc. Then, leave the notes somewhere the other partner will find them.

Lifestyle exercises

Sometimes, relationships wilt under the daily onslaught of chores, work, money, child rearing - here are exercises that focus on reorienting your relationship as a daily priority.

The play date

Decide on something fun you can both do together. This doesn't have to be anything serious like taking up a dance class - if you both like board games or rolling down hills in the park, then that's what you do. The trick is: both of you must enjoy it. Work together; have fun.

Role swap

For the day, act out the part of your partner - pretend to be them in every way. Treat them the way you feel treated by them. Speak, think and act like them. Your partner does the same. Are they accurate? What do they think of your rendition? How do you interact when you are, well, them?

Opposite day

Both of you commit you to saying *exactly the opposite* of what you want to say. In an argument? Instead of saying, "Ugh, I've had enough of this", say "I want nothing more than to keep on doing this." Instead of saying, "You're wrong", say *"I'm* wrong". Your partner does the same. What happens?

Make a ritual

Decide on something that you and your partner can do today every day, something ritualistic. It doesn't matter what - just that you keep up the ritual for the remainder of the days. Maybe you read to each other from the newspaper, brush your teeth together before starting the day or call each other every day at lunchtime.

Communication exercises

The following exercises are for strengthening you and your partner's ability to really reach one another and open up healthy channels of communication.

The sound of silence

For the day, communicate with your partner only through body language and facial expression. You can talk to others, but when together, you can only make yourself understood through your body, smile and eyes. How good are you?

Nursing home letters

Imagine you are on your deathbed, about to shuffle off this mortal coil and at the end of a long, full life. Write a letter to your partner. Make it as long or as short as you like. Imagine what you'd say to them after all is said and done, your parting words, your goodbye. What do you say? How does it feel to read your partner's letter to you?

Communicative gifts

Exchange small gifts. Make the gift symbolic and communicative. You don't need to discuss the meaning, just find creative ways to non-verbally put your message out there. You can do whatever you like: a wilted flower, a polished stone, a specific book, a handful of pills, a pile of dog poo wrapped in beautiful paper?

Daily reading

Every day, as you wake, take an emotional "reading" of your partner. Take turns, and tell them how you perceive them that day. Are they exhausted, content, defensive, affectionate? Compare notes and see if you both improve with time.

Conflict exercises

Keeping the ratio right

In all your communications for the day, try to balance every criticism or negative thing with *four* positive ones or compliments. This will slow things down, but do it anyway. Make your compliments sincere. "You have such beautiful hands. I love the way you always cook lasagna so perfectly. You have great taste in movies. I love your jokes. I think it's gross that you leave your towel on the floor like that."

"That's OK"

For one day, accept whatever conflicts arise with you and your partner. They say something stupid or disrespectful? That's OK. You don't agree, even a little? That's OK. Resist trying to solve anything, or trying to change the other one's mind. Look squarely at the conflict and say, in your spirit, *that's OK*. How does it feel to be this accepting?

Practicing acceptance

This exercise can be done alone by you and your partner. Write down everything that you wish you could change about your partner, everything that you think is wrong with them. Now crumple up the paper or burn it to smithereens. Make the vow to accept them for who they are, right now, without any amendments.

Calling time-outs

If your relationship is fraught with bickering, arguments and petty fights, institute a "timeout" strategy. The moment one of you senses a fight coming on, somebody is obliged to call a time-out. After this, both of you take the time to gather your thoughts, take a breather and come back to the issue an hour later.

Day 27: Appraisal

If you've missioned through the full 30 days, engaged the participation of your partner and been thorough and honest with yourself in your diary, you'll have a lot of new experiences to draw on as the 30 days comes to an end.

Go back and look at your original goals, fears and expectations. What has changed? How do you feel now about the issues you had going in? Try to explore what new things you have learnt about your partner in the process.

What habits from the 30 days do you want to keep into the future, and what habits do you want to definitely drop from your repertoire? It may be difficult, but you may have decided to end or dramatically change the course of your relationship.

Where do you want to go from here?

Day 28 and 29: Cool-off

Rest and process. Take a step back and allow your thoughts to develop fully.

Day 30: Projection

Try to summarize the experience of the last month. Write a journal entry and speak to your partner about their experience. If it feels natural, decide on how you'd like to move forward. Do you have new goals? New energy to commit to a different lifestyle?

Chapter 7: Troubleshooting for the 30 days

- *"My partner thinks all of this is lame and won't play along"*

And, what do you make of the fact that there is this difference between you? It might help in the short term to be the one doing all the work, but will you be happy for the long term to be the only one instigating change? Some of these exercises are awkward and difficult. But do you want to be with someone who isn't even really willing to try?

- *"Actually, I'm the one who is uncomfortable doing some of these things"*

Discomfort is not the end of the world. Can you embark on something new and strange with good humor and resilience? Can you be light and easy about it? At the very least, try. Not every exercise will benefit you, or make sense for your situation. Write down in your diary whether you're resistant just because you are afraid of what you might uncover or whether you genuinely feel uninspired. If you find yourself rejecting one particular exercise strongly, it's a good sign that there's something there worth your attention. Whether you end up doing it or not, what does the exercise show you?

- *"What if we break up?"*

Well, what if you do? Ending a relationship that is not healthy or working is not a failure, it's a step in the right direction. In a sense, your goal is not to make sure you and your partner get on perfectly, it's trying to find that sweet spot where your hopes and goals coincide with your partner's, where your intentions both align. Sometimes, the best thing people can do for each other is to sever their connection. Always ask - are you serving one another's highest good? Any movement in this direction is something to be celebrated, not feared or avoided.

Conclusion

When it really comes down to it, the relationships we have with others are just extensions of the relationship we have with ourselves. In the same way that you wouldn't and shouldn't accept someone who is unclear on their goals, unable to communicate well and unwilling to open up and be vulnerable, so you should work hard at not being that person yourself.

True love, soul mates and love at first sight may or may not be worthwhile topics of discussion, but even the best and strongest love needs the watchful care and maintenance of two healthy, mature people to keep it going. Compassionate communication is part of this.

I hope that in this book, you've been able to unearth some interesting new things about yourself, and discovered a renewed sense of your own values, your own purpose and your own goals when it comes to love. And if you have, I hope that you've been inspired to communicate that more freely and honestly to those around you.

Finally, I would like to take this opportunity to thank you for deciding to pick up this book among all the other books out there. If you've benefited from reading this book, I would so love to hear in what ways it has helped you. You can leave a review for this book by searching for the title of this book on www.amazon.com.

Bonus Preview: Codependency - "Loves Me, Loves Me Not": Learn How To Cultivate Healthy Relationships, Overcome Relationship Jealousy, Stop Controlling Others and Be Codependent No More

If you've had difficulty with starting or maintaining relationships, issues with feeling jealous and possessive or find that your connections with others are more a source of distress than anything else, this book is for you.

By finding ways to be more mindful throughout the day, as well as exercises in improving your communication skills, this book will show you how to have relationships that are calmer and more stable and compassionate.

We'll begin with a look at the phenomenon of codependency, what it has traditionally meant in the psychological realm and how these traits and patterns can be traced back to issues of self-worth, compassion and more deliberate action. We'll examine how mindfulness can be the magic ingredient to getting a hold of the codependency cycle, and some of the characteristics of happy, mindful relationships. Finally, we'll explore a model for mindful communication and ways that you can begin to implement immediately in order to make a commitment to stronger, more compassionate relationships with others.

It may feel sometimes that an intense and serious connection with someone is proof of the depth of the feeling you have for one another. But be careful, obsession and dependency is not the same as love. In the codependent relationship, our affection and attention is coming from a place of fear and need. As a result, the partners never really connect with each other. They do endless, complicated dances around each others problems, but what they never do is make an honest human connection.

In codependent relationships, manipulation, guilt and resentment take the place of healthy, balanced affection. Codependent partners are not necessarily together because they want to be, they are because they have to be, because they don't know how to live otherwise. One partner may bring a history of abuse, a "personality disorder" or mental illness into a relationship; the ways the other partner responds to this may be healthy or not, but if they bring their own issues to the table too, they may find that the bond of their love is more accurately described as a shared and complementary dysfunction.

Remember, the relationships we are in can never be better than the relationships we have with ourselves. Two unhappy people together never make a happy couple together. We cannot treat other people in ways we have never taken the time to consider before, and we cannot communicate properly if we are not even sure what it is we need to communicate in the first place.

An individual with a mature, well-developed sense of themselves has the most to offer someone else. They have their own lives, their own sense of self-worth, their own strength. And when you remove need, fear, obsession and desperation, you open up the way for love and affection just for its own sake.

Love is many things, but it's cheapened when held hostage by the ego. Connections formed around ego and fear may be strong and lasting, but what keeps them going is mutual need. What could be more romantic than, "I don't need to be with you. You don't complete me at all. I am happy and stable and fulfilled without you. But I still want to be with you, because you're awesome"?

On the ground, in the nitty gritty of life, we can reduce a massive thing like "Relationships" down to smaller, more manageable units. Everything from the deepest and most profound romantic and spiritual union to sharing a joke with the cashier at the supermarket rests on one thing: communication. Whether it's through words or not, we are constantly communicating, and the accumulation of these little units creates this big thing we call a relationship.

Other Books By This Author

- Self-Compassion - I Don't Have To Feel Better Than Others To Feel Good About Myself: Learn How To See Self Esteem Through The Lens Of Self-Love and Mindfulness and Cultivate The Courage To Be You

- How To Stop Worrying and Start Living - What Other People Think Of Me Is None Of My Business: Learn Stress Management and How To Overcome Relationship Jealousy, Social Anxiety and Stop Being Insecure

- Codependency - "Loves Me, Loves Me Not": Learn How To Cultivate Healthy Relationships, Overcome Relationship Jealousy, Stop Controlling Others and Be Codependent No More

- Mindful Eating: A Healthy, Balanced and Compassionate Way To Stop Overeating, How To Lose Weight and Get a Real Taste of Life by Eating Mindfully

- Minimalism: How to Declutter, De-Stress and Simplify Your Life With Simple Living

- The Minimalist Budget: A Practical Guide On How To Save Money, Spend Less And Live More With A Minimalist Lifestyle

- Self-Esteem for Kids – Every Parent's Greatest Gift: How To Raise Kids To Have Confidence In Themselves And Their Own Abilities

Made in the USA
San Bernardino, CA
23 May 2017